I0816752

PHOTOGRAPHS
TOM SHEEHAN

ESSAYS
CRAIG McLEAN

For Jamie, Alex and Florrie X

Thanks to...
Ed O'Brien and Radiohead
Courtyard Management
Carl Glover
Craig McLean
Joe Cottington
Caffy St Luce
Murray Chalmers
Lesley Bleakley
Florence Pick
Regent Sounds

TS 2024

CONTENTS

CONTENTS

FOREWORD

When I look at Tom's photos of us they start, appropriately, in Oxford, on Keble Road, in 1992 and end up eleven years later in NYC, which also feels kind of appropriate. It reflects the kind of journey that we went on in those years and, coincidentally or not, Tom was often with us, snapping away at some of those defining moments. The first ever shoot for the *Melody Maker*. Our first visit to America and LA. The launch of *OK Computer* to the world in Tokyo and Barcelona. The Tibetan Freedom Concert in '98. Taking *Kid A* out onto the road. These were all big moments for us, and he was there because we trusted him. And he was good.

We didn't let many in, partly because we could be awkward buggers, but also because the only thing we were interested in was making good music, getting better at our craft and connecting with our audience through shows. That, believe it or not, didn't endear us to the British music press initially. Oh, and also the fact that we were all from middle class backgrounds, which at the beginning of the '90s was definitely something to kick a young band about. But Tom never did. He never judged us, and with every session our friendship and trust grew ever greater.

You realize as you get older that the journey is everything. Yes, of course success can be a wonderful thing, but it's the way you get there that counts, and with that some of the people that you meet and share these moments with. Tom is one of them. A beautiful man and a beautiful photographer.

Thank you, Tom.
With huge gratitude and love,

ED

INTRODUCTION

I have had the pleasure of working with Radiohead for more than a decade, during which time they went from a new band to something truly inspirational.

I remember shooting them on the roof of the Capitol Records building in LA on one of our early sessions together, in 1993. They were just young guys then, putting in the hours with the salespeople, press and radio DJs etc, to try to build something. Now, thirty-odd years later, they've earned the right to stand on the roof of that building as one of the biggest bands in the world.

Over that time we've become not old friends as such, but old comrades. We've had a good working relationship, I think in part because I worked with them so early on, when they were still finding out who they were and in particular how they wanted to present themselves in photographs. But they're also great people on an individual level. We might go a few years without working together, but when we do meet we can just pick up where we left off last time, sharing and recommending records, books, etc.

Radiohead are an inspirational band, so incredibly talented and creative, but they also look to what others do for their own inspiration. When I met up with Ed not long ago he gave me an Arthur Verocai album – payback, he said, for a David Crosby album I'd given him at some point. The band is like that, always fired-up by culture and on the lookout for interesting ideas and approaches. They give me not just inspiration to seek out these things myself, but also a thirst to keep going, to pick these things up. They won't tell you to go out and read this, listen to that, but if you're perceptive then just being around them is enough to pick things up anyway. A creative osmosis...

They're often seen as a serious band. And they are, their music is deep and thoughtful. But funnily enough, when I think of working with them I see them laughing. When you're working, of course they have to put on a professional face, as we all do. It's been great to see them develop as a band, but also in our work together. In our early sessions they were unsure, still finding their image. But in our later shoots, though I'm still directing, they know what to do now.

They're one of the most interesting bands I've ever worked with, not just for their music but also for what they ignite in me.

Tom Sheehan

LONDON:

"Uh, heh-heh, what is this?" asks a teenager, as confused as he is pimply, as he watches an unseen video by an unknown band play on his television.

"Don't worry, Butt-Head," replies Beavis, sitting next to him on the sofa, "it gets cool in a minute."

"It better start rocking," grumps Butt-Head, eyeballing the singer, "or I'll really give him something to cry about."

Beavis tells him to shut up – the pasty English guy on TV with the choirboy voice and shaggy, bleached-blonde hair is just warming up. Then, from out of their telly it comes: a huge, jagged, furniture-shifting guitar riff. The kids explode from their couch in a frenzy of head-banging, fist-pumping and very-metal exultation.

"RAAAAAH!" shouts Beavis. "*Yeah yeah yeah yeah!*"

Butt-Head has changed his mind. "This is pretty cool!"

Then, suddenly, the song changes again. To their adolescent minds it's gone back to being soft. To being uncool. "What…?" splutters Beavis. "What's going on? How come they don't just, like, play that cool part through the whole song?"

Ah, the mid-nineties. When MTV was a defining force in culture and the "M" in its name stood for "music", not mindless reality TV tat. When the channel's resident advisers – a pair of spotty, snotty, oiky, badly drawn boys in an American animation – were the culture-defining arbiters of what was hot and what was not. And for British bands trying to make a dent in the US, Mike Judge's *Beavis & Butt-Head* was as brutal as it was basic as it was brilliant. You had to laugh. If you didn't, you might cry, pack up and go back to shuffling around the UK's indie circuit.

But if you had greater ambitions than that, you had to learn to take your cartoon licks, because undoubtedly things would get immeasurably tougher. Viewing your breakthrough anthem "Creep" as an albatross around your necks – a song you'd ultimately banish from your setlist for years at a time – wouldn't even be the half of it. Meeting people is easy? Hardly.

But right now?

"It's so cool to get on a programme like *Beavis and Butt-Head*," Radiohead's Thom Yorke is telling me in a hotel in central London. "That was great. My favourite bit is where Beavis goes, 'if they didn't have a bit of the song that sucked, then the other bit wouldn't be so great.' Yes!" the singer exclaims, cheerfully.

I ask if it might be the best review Radiohead have had for "Creep", the single whose success – number 7 in the UK, a smash in a couple of dozen countries – hauled them round the world on an endless world tour. Okay, it actually lasted just shy of two years, but having been originally released a year before it was a hit, Campaign Creep had been very long indeed.

"Yes, absolutely. Wonderful!" Thom, at the time of the interview 26 years old, replies chirpily. "He should write for the music press. Once you've been on *Beavis and Butt-Head*…"

…you've arrived?

"Absolutely."

Even if they're taking the piss?

"Oh, yeah. We take ourselves far too seriously sometimes."

JANUARY 1995

I'm not gonna lie: in early 1995 I may have been Butt-Head-adjacent.

Radiohead were far from a big, or important, or must-listen-to band for me at that time. I'd seen them live, on Friday 30 October 1992, at The Venue, a tiny club in Edinburgh. They'd only been signed in Christmas week 1991, under their original name of On A Friday, their rock'n'roll nomenclature taken from the day – oh yes – on which they rehearsed. Little wonder, then, that that autumn, as demonstrated by the photographs taken by Tom Sheehan in their home town of Oxford the previous month, the band were floppy, bashful and trying on for size what it felt like to be a band. Sunglasses? Check. Leather jacket? Check. Staring meaningfully into the distance? We can do that!

Edinburgh was one stop on the now-legendary tour where the five-piece from Oxford supported not only up-and-coming Hull trio Kingmaker but also the juggler who was onstage between Radiohead and the headliners. "Creep" had been released for the first time the previous month but neither it nor the band's set that night registered much with me. Me and my student mates did, though, snicker at the very Spinal Tap-ness of their billing.

History does not record whether any balls were dropped that cold evening in the Scottish capital, but certainly over the next year or so it seemed like Radiohead spilled a few of their own. Their debut album, *Pablo Honey*, came out in February 1993. It felt thin. Basic. Another British guitar album released in the dead zone between the fag-end of grunge and the birth-spasms of Britpop. Not as good as Catherine Wheel.

Even when, eventually, "Creep" crept inexorably around the world, dragging *Pablo Honey* behind it to the tune of 1.1 million copies purchased in less than two years – and a gold disc in the Philippines – I wasn't sold.

Then, in January 1995 I was contacted by a commissioning editor at "CD magazine" *Volume*: would I like to interview Radiohead? As an eager-beaver-cub journalist, my first instinct was: "Where do you want me?" My second instinct: "Ah, yeah, but I'm not really into them…" Then again, it was a chance to travel to London. For this rookie writer, desperate for some national profile, it had the whiff of a Proper Assignment, even if I didn't wholeheartedly view Radiohead as a Proper Band. Yes, I'm afraid I was that snotty.

Then I received an advance cassette of Radiohead's second album, which was the reason for the interview – *The Bends.*

But was this really the same people? I couldn't believe what I was hearing. From the very opening, the echoing thrum of "Planet Telex", this was an entirely different band. As if a group of schoolfriends who'd been pinballed round the world had grabbed that head-spinning energy and chaos between their collective hands and forced them into the very atoms of their songwriting. Nuclear (con)fusion. It was that powerful.

To be fair (to me), Radiohead seemed just as perplexed by this turn of events.

"It was really hard to get any judgement on the second album," says Thom on that wintry day 29 years ago. "There was a lot of tearing ourselves to bits – and tearing what we were doing to bits as well, because we had so much to prove."

Prefiguring the industry-shaking battles Radiohead would be having a decade or so hence, they admit that their record company – surprise – didn't wholly help either.

"You go from being a band that's pretty inconsequential on EMI's worldwide roster to being up there as a priority alongside Pink Floyd," says guitarist Ed O'Brien.

"The worst thing," adds fellow guitarist Jonny Greenwood – the man whose playing on "Creep" knocked America off its collective couch and, later, would require the guitarist to wear a wrist-brace onstage – "is that we felt, creatively, in a kind of stasis for a year and a half because we couldn't release anything new. Three months ago we were still supporting *Pablo Honey* in

Mexico. Which is fine, but it just perpetuated the idea that we've got no other songs – just because we haven't had the time to do anything new."

He rues the elongated, attenuated focus on *Pablo Honey*, an enervating global schlep that had robbed Radiohead of their original, concise, perhaps naïve plan: release one album then "the second one would be done straight away, really. Maybe do two tours in the UK in between – certainly not leave Britain, maybe go to France or something. But it just got stretched out and out and out." He sighs. "When six years ago we'd been a band who'd be writing and recording and playing in front of no one, just for fun."

I ask the pair of guitarists if travelling the world and shifting over a million copies of their debut album had robbed them of that fun.

"Completely," Jonny shoots back.

"No," says Ed, already revealing himself to be one of the more unflappable members of the band.

Then Jonny backtracks, a bit. "It did for me sometimes. A little bit. It's fun to play concerts, but looking ahead it can be very bleak."

Just you wait, my time-travelling self thinks in January '95. *This summer I'm going to meet you all in Dallas, at the Starplex Amphitheatre, while you're supporting R.E.M. on their monster* Monster *tour of American "sheds". That'll learn you about the bleakness of touring. And in two years we're going to meet again, in Barcelona, where a pair of club shows to launch* OK Computer *will tee up an epochal Glastonbury performance in mudbound June '97 – and then the bleakness will really dig in.*

Still, it seems the 1995 model of Radiohead has a sense of the way the wind is blowing. Their first album was named after a sketch by telephone pranksters The Jerky Boys. Their second after the decompression sickness caused by a rapid change in pressure.

They describe to me how 1994 and the making of *The Bends* should have gone, if their plans had worked out. At the start of the year, six weeks holiday. Studio time in March with producer John Leckie in RAK in North London, with five potential singles being demanded early on of this Pink Floyd-level priority. Finished and out of the studio in early May in time for a tour of the Far East and Australia. Back home for a mid-summer release of the now-completed album. Then a late-summer, pre-autumn tour of America. And onwards, ever onwards, with the campaign.

But the RAK sessions were "tentative", "clinical" and "unspontaneous". Or, as Ed puts it: "At the end of last March, we'd been recording for four weeks and it sounded like a turkey." Having almost torn themselves apart once before, during a month-long tour of America with Belly in autumn 1993, Radiohead were again fraying at the edges.

But on the stages of Australian and New Zealand clubs, they rediscovered their purpose and focus. New songs "The Bends" and "Bones" landed brilliantly. Returning to the UK, the band scrapped all the previous recordings and booked into The Manor Studio in Oxfordshire. They banged out *The Bends* in two weeks.

"We started off recording *The Bends* like paranoid little mice in cages," reflects Thom. "We were so frightened, so shit-scared about getting this record right. Every act and every note we played was a real major deal. To go from that to feeling like we were back in Jonny's bedroom doing what the fuck we wanted – that's what makes this record special."

Talking to me again later, he recalls the moment he first heard a test-pressing of the album that would change his life and launch Radiohead on the way to being the 20th-century's Last Great Rock Band – and the early 21st-century's most consistently, contrarily, disruptively and devastatingly inventive.

"I thought: *this is it*. This is what it was all about in the first place. We've come out of all this more alive than we ever were when we went in. That's what I feel like. It's just like we're starting fresh again."

Hang on, Thom. Hang on to that feeling. Because eight months from now, you and I will be sitting under blazing Texan sunshine, during the third of four American tours for Radiohead in the year of our dog 1995. And you will be telling me about a dinner conversation you had with your current touring partner, Michael Stipe, viz:

"I find it alarming, the sort of things that happen to him. As a magnet for all sorts of bizarre debris, people, nutters. He was saying he had a really difficult time on the *Green* tour, where he didn't quite want this to happen actually.

"What Stipe does is immerse himself in it. He reads everything that's written about them. Which is what I used to do. But I found there was so much bad I couldn't read it. I had to stop reading all of it. Personally, I've had things written about me that have really, really hurt. It's not actually that nice to be called ugly more than ten times in a year in the press. I didn't get into this fucking business because I was beautiful."

We will, undoubtedly, come back to that.

OXFORD:

This was my first encounter with the band. There was a vibe around “Creep” before it went ballistic, so I was dispatched up to shoot them for a small feature. We met in the Jericho Tavern, a pub they used to play in back when they were called On A Friday. As with a lot of new bands, I think there was a slight reluctance to having their photograph taken, which is fair enough – for any young band, unless they’re those types that set themselves on fire, it can be uncomfortable for them, they don’t want to do it. So I felt they needed a little direction, but not too much. We went for a wander towards the Pitt Rivers Museum and saw this great mural of a creature and a note in massive letters next to it: “remember what happened to the dinosaur”. A warning for any band! Perhaps over the course of their career as they pushed to break musical boundaries they were glancing over their shoulder at that sign on the wall, who knows?

The shoot was great. It was short, sharp and swift but we got some nice introductory pictures of the band. Ed kindly gave me a lift back to Oxford train station and I remember he was plugging me about all the times I’d worked with REM – a year later they were on tour with them.

SEPTEMBER 1992

REMEMBER WHAT
HAPPENED TO THE
DINOSAUR!

Bison bison
American Bison
Presented by Lord Wharncliffe, 1868.
No. 17430

CLICK STUDIOS LONDON:

After our first encounter in Oxford, which had a real ease about it, I was asked by the record company to go and take the band's first proper publicity pictures. They were signed to Parlophone, part of EMI, so a huge label, but the band didn't want all the razzmatazz that usually comes with that. They didn't want to be made up and dressed like a corporate rock band, so apparently they worked out a deal where they were each given 500 quid and allowed to spend it on whatever clobber they liked. Colin went out and blew his entire budget on a Paul Smith suit, which you can see half of here. You might think that's quite expensive, but the chap wore it for the next two and half years, so it was money well spent! The session started off quite slowly; we took a few pictures of the band and it wasn't quite working somehow. So we stopped for a cup of tea and took a walk, and tried again. In time they relaxed, a slow realization dawned that I came in peace.

These early shoots together can be a hard thing for a young band, especially a thoughtful band like Radiohead, to swallow. You can imagine why – they're having their identity taken away from them before they've even formed it. But we persevered

OCTOBER 1992

and this session was a good one. It helped form the basis of a resulting ten-odd years working together, and it was down to being understanding of them as people, not as a product.

HORNSEY BATHS LONDON:

I was asked to document a video shoot, with the idea that I might be able to capture something that would work for the cover of *Pablo Honey*. The band were recording a video in Hornsey Baths, a Victorian swimming pool and laundry which had been empty for years. But when I arrived, Thom told me they'd already settled on the cover, an illustration. Which was fine by me, and just as well – I'm not sure how you can shoot an album cover in the 30 seconds you get in between takes! Though it could actually work well, if the batteries were charged and Thom was already throwing shapes for the video then it made sense that he would be up for it – if he wasn't already knackered.

So I grabbed what I could, shooting the band against the tiles, and we got some lovely pictures, some of which ended up on the inside of the album sleeve. I love the photograph of Ed down in the pool, holding up his guitar with "Pablo Honey" on it, and the one of Thom in the pool with the chicken or turkey or whatever it was. They were all taken on the hoof, when they were recording the video.

NOVEMBER 1992

PABLO
HONEY

OXFORD:

I met the chaps in Oxford again, this time to shoot a feature for *Melody Maker* for their second single, "Anyone Can Play Guitar", hence the portraits with the band's hands on the guitar. We kicked off at Thom's flat. He lived in the bottom half of a house on Iffley Road, and Radiohead being arty boys, had a nice Rothko poster on the wall. We went out and about – someone had some grand plans to get onto the roof of a big clocktower somewhere in the centre of town. But it became clear there wasn't enough space for five band members plus me to clamber about several storeys up, so we knocked that on the head quite quickly and instead rattled off some frames in a shopping centre.

JANUARY 1993

SALE
SALE
SALE
SALE

RICHARDS
SALE
SALE
SALE
SALE

PABLO HONEY
PABLO HONEY
PABLO HONEY

PABLO
HONEY

es County Museum
Cindy Crawford
wants it all
From Gore to eternity

Los Angeles County Museum of
ROTHKO
Cindy Crawford
wants it all

LOS ANGELES:

The band were out in LA to do a massive US press push – radio was king back then in the States, so they were holed up in the Capitol Records building talking on the blower to everyone: salespeople, DJs, journos and whoever from Arizona to Alaska. There was also a big lunch for all of the salespeople. They were working hard with the key players in the record business, and the effort paid off – after all, it was college radio that really helped break them out there.

I was out to shoot a feature with them, and before they got too busy I suggested we go up to the roof of the building to get a few shots. I was actually suffering from horrendous vertigo, but the boys didn't seem to mind, and nor did Thom, who – sorry, Thom – was the focus of the session at the time. For newer bands especially, it's a kind of visual shorthand to focus in on the singer, so there are always more shots of him than the other chaps.

At some point the kind people at Capitol thought it would be nice to reward the band by giving us all access to the Blue Note Records cupboard, full of jazz treasures. We stripped it bare before they kicked us out. Their next single was "Pop

APRIL 1993

Is Dead", hence me scribbling that on the cover of a *USA Today* and getting Jonny to hold it in the background of a few shots on the street outside, through gritted teeth, admittedly.

I think for the band, when you're strangers in a strange land, even relatively familiar faces like I was by then become someone you react well to. And I was trying to do my best by them, making sure I got as much as possible from the trip, which is why I grabbed Thom while we were waiting around to go out for the evening and got him to snap a few images on the Sunset Strip.

Of course, the band probably didn't know what I was up to at the time, I was just getting on their nerves! I think they were happy to be getting away from those radio interviews for a bit though.

GIFT WRAP
KEYS
8491
MAIL BOXES
UPS
AUTHORIZED
UPS
D.S.H. Delivery
& Messenger Service
310-657-2993
SHIPPI
MAILBOX
RENTALS
VOICE MAIL
24 HR.
MESSAGE CENTER
LOCAL TELEPHONE
POP DEAD
UPS Air Services
Available Here.
Ask Us.
Next Day Air
2nd Day Air
Worldwide Services

KEYS
THORIZED
D.S.H. Deliver
& Messenger Se
310-657
MAILBO
RENTALS
VOICE MA
24 HR.
MESSAGE CEN
LOCAL TELEP

MUSIC 72

MUSIC 72

MUSIC 72

BOSTON + NYC:

I'd been in LA, but flew over on the red-eye to see Radiohead playing a club, I think supporting Belly, at the Avalon in Boston. Before the gig we went outside to do a few quick set ups – Jonny was reading Miles Davis' autobiography at the time, with every third word being "motherfucker", so that kept things interesting. A genius inspiring a bunch of geniuses.

I don't think I'd seen them play live before, but the gig was brilliant – they were throwing some great shapes which made for really interesting pictures. They were inclined to do that on stage, their style being so informed by grunge at that time, but they really went for it. It was explosive – this was early in their career of course so at that point in time they had a lot to prove. I rattled off a few frames backstage afterwards. You can see that they were starting to get an early following, as people were beginning to ask for their autographs.

Then we moved on to New York. We went out a few times over the weekend but for one of our sessions I went out with them after they'd just shot a piece for some high-end fashion magazine. Some

OCTOBER 1993

of them had kept on their outfits so they were in some distinctly non-Radiohead clobber. Thom had a gold lamé jacket involved at some point, but that was quickly ditched, more's the pity.

The band were obliging through all of this, but you can see from some of the shots – by the "do not enter" sign especially – that their patience is starting to wear thin. I haven't a clue why I asked them to burn a dollar bill, it's just one of those things you do to spark some visual interest.

6-R

14 OF 21
RADIOHE
STAGE
LEFT

dw

RADIO
HEAD

S·I·R
RADIO
HEAD

BAR
LOUNGE
Bill's
BAR
LOUNGE
Miles

BAR
LOUNGE
Bill's
BAR
LOUNG
BACK BA
PRINTING
COMPANY
5
Miles

LOUNG

DO NOT
ENTER

DRIVE-IN
DINER

DRIVE-IN
DINER

BARCELONA:

"Radiohead have created an album motivated and unified by one overriding theme: three years away from the millennium, Yorke wants to leave the planet and escape from the routine and clutter of life... every track on OK Computer *is driven by a feeling of impotence with the world around it... ages-defining and one of the most startling albums... this is not only 1997's finest moment by several miles, but it may well prove to be one of the finest albums humanity has ever seen... I do not know how to describe what is essentially an indescribable sound, but I had one last idea while watching the very English spectacle of Princess Diana's funeral... this is a landmark... 'Bohemian Rhapsody'...* The Dark Side of the Moon*... ambitious... edgy... psycho-drama... pretentious twaddle.... truly this is one of the greatest albums in living memory – and one that distances them from their peers by an interstellar mile..."*

The vultures – and the smudges – are circling. Radiohead are in Barcelona to launch *OK Computer*. The day after the initial, Japanese release of their third album, they're playing two shows, on 22 and 24 May, at Zeleste, a club with a capacity of around 2,000. It's almost four weeks until the record's UK release, six before it hits the US. But already it feels too small. Already it feels too hot.

To anyone who had imagined that following the world-beating crunch of *The Bends* with a quasi-conceptual, prog-rock treatise on alienation, consumerism, factory farming, the IMF and British arms exports – to name but a fistful of the planet-sized ills ailing 28-year-old Thom Yorke – would have tapered the vertiginous excitement around the band: your imagination, clearly, wasn't up to that of Radiohead.

Because already the press pack present in the Spanish city – the ones privileged enough to have received advance copies of the album, encased in promotional jiffy bags block-stamped with the words to the album's Stephen Hawking-like spoken-word interlude "Fitter Happier" – know that *OK Computer* is a masterpiece. Is it really, though, to quote one of the screeds of atomically glowing reviews, one of the finest albums that humanity has ever seen?

Even the twitchy agit-jitters of the about-to-be-released "Paranoid Android", a single that comprises four sections, runs to almost six-and-half minutes and that will give Radiohead their biggest British hit (#3), couldn't have OK-computed that kind of epoch-making billing.

Certainly, Radiohead are now playing by their own rules. Ones that have nothing to do with grunge and post-grunge, Britpop and shitpop, and everything to do with listening to Can and Morricone and Miles Davis' *Bitches Brew*, fuming at the evening news, spewing at the spiralling world, collaborating with new producer Nigel Godrich, spending £100,000 of label Parlophone's money on recording equipment, and giving it some to kicking, squealing Gucci little piggies.

And now, again already, everyone likes those rules. Not bad for an album that was partly road-tested on a sunny summer American tour supporting Alanis Morissette.

Barcelona, accordingly, is *a scrum*. On the day in between the two kick-off shows, celebrations for drummer Phil Selway's thirtieth birthday are way down the order of business – one that runs to seven itinerized pages of international media commitments and obligations. Magazine teams, TV crews, radio DJs, documentarians. Interview after interview. Photoshoot after photoshoot. Reporters report on other reporters. Cameras capture cameras. Who watches the watchers? Other watchers!

For the benefit of the few representatives of the world's media apparently *not* on the ground for this global press event, there's even a proto-internet press conference. You can imagine the dial-up modem *skreeee* and *clang-chirp-clang*. Alas, it collapses under the weight of online fan intrusion. Funny that.

Thom loses his mind listening to a French interviewer, who wangs on incessantly about "Creep". The man from American muso mag *Musician* causes a tetchy argument between Phil, Ed and bass player Colin Greenwood when he asks about

MAY 1997

"the intricate guitar line in 5/4 time" that opens new song "Let Down". My time with the band goes down the toilet: on assignment for *THE FACE*, our slot amounts to five minutes in the bogs, wherein our photographer shoots Jonny and Ed in plastic patio chairs, Phil and Colin by the washbasins, and Thom poised by a cubicle door, as if ready to bolt inside and flush the whole thing.

Tom Sheehan, of course, has much better luck and access, getting the band out into the street and picturing them (mostly) without the mobs of excitable hovering fans.

Thirty-five days after Barcelona, Radiohead top the Pyramid Stage on the middle night of Glastonbury. Defying the sucking mud and appalling sound that has an angry Thom briefly vacating the stage, they deliver one of the festival's all-time great headline performances. Lucky for those of us standing on the hill at Worthy Farm, braving the howling elements and hearing eight of *OK Computer*'s tracks, beginning, at the top of the set, appropriately enough, with "Lucky"...

... because "Lucky" was a cornerstone of what would become *OK Computer*. It was written during what Ed would later characterize as "a good time", in the summer immediately following the May 1995 release of *The Bends*. "It was classic [and] this is why it's important to be throwaway," the guitarist tells me in 2001. "We had an album out for two months, we were going back into the studio to do B-sides... Yeah, our fans listen to B-sides, but there was no pressure."

Those writing sessions produced "Bishop's Robes" and "Talk Show Host", both of which appeared as the B-sides of January 1996 *Bends* single "Street Spirit (Fade Out)". "Talk Show Host" would also appear on the soundtrack to Baz Luhrmann's *Romeo + Juliet*, released in November 1996. Reinforcing Ed's conviction that an un-pressured band is a creative band, in those sessions they also wrote "Lucky".

It found a home quicker than Radiohead could have imagined. On 4 September 1995, *The Help Album* was recorded: one day, 20 tracks, multiple artists in myriad studios, to raise funds for War Child, the charity that helps civilians suffering in war zones such as (at the time) the former Yugoslavia. Approached by co-founder Brian Eno to be involved, Radiohead offered up "Lucky". No B-side, this: this track was the unassuming yet magisterial beginning of Radiohead Phase #3. Enlisting Godrich (John Leckie's engineer on *The Bends*) as producer, they recorded the song in five hours.

Five days later, on 9 September, *The Help Album* was in the shops.

Eleven days after that, on 20 September 1995, I saw Radiohead supporting R.E.M. at Dallas's Starplex Amphitheatre. "Lucky" was already front-and-centre, its position at the heart of the opening act's necessarily tight, eight-song set a mark of its onrushing importance to the band. I spoke to Thom a few hours before showtime, both of us sitting on the venue's "lawn" area as Berry, Buck, Mills and Stipe soundchecked on the open-air stage. It was clear that he was already wrestling with where Radiohead now found themselves – playing 20,000-capacity American "sheds" (albeit as the opening act) – and where they were headed next.

"It's a weird situation to be in," he said, swaddled in black in defiance of the fierce Texan heat, "to be the stadium rock band it's okay to like." But their love of "the whole Phil Spector thing, huge-sounding instruments" wasn't just big for big's sake. "For me it's so much more evocative. It's not because we want to change the world... [I]t's a reaction against everything else we're hearing. Not really in Britain, Britain is diverse enough for you not to have to react against it, there's enough going on. But over here everything's exactly the same, everything's dry. That whole inverted integrity about having everything completely in your face. Which I find [means] nothing left to the imagination whatsoever."

Little wonder, perhaps, that "Lucky" – a chiming, spectral ballad that builds to a magnificent, heads-thrown-back howl – was already emerging as pathfinder for what Radiohead would do next. As Thom would later characterize it to *Musician*, the song was "the first mark on the wall".

Radiohead's touring schedule in 1995 was relentless. It ran practically non-stop from 10 February (The Lomax, Liverpool) to 18 December (Universal Amphitheatre, Los Angeles), via that R.E.M. run. The success of *The Bends* propelled the band, feet barely touching the ground, from a 300-capacity Merseyside club to the 6th Annual KROQ Almost Acoustic Christmas jamboree alongside Bush, Morissette and Lenny Kravitz.

By January 1996 the band were in dire need of a break, and spent the month at home in Oxfordshire recording demos for their third album. By mid-March, they were out on the road again, slogging round (mostly) America until the end of August. But by that summer they were trying out new songs, with "Electioneering" and "Paranoid Android" possibly not offering the sweetness expected by Morissette fans at Hersheypark Stadium in Hershey, Pennsylvania, home of the Great American Chocolate Bar.

They'd also reconnected with Luhrmann. The film director commissioned them for another song for his *Romeo + Juliet* soundtrack. The Australian, a fabulist with fabulous attention to detail, let the band see the final 30 minutes' footage. Inspired by the image of Claire Danes' Juliet, the silver-tone Para-Ordnance pistol of lover Romeo (Leonardo DiCaprio) pressed to her temple, the band began writing what would become "Exit Music (For a Film)". It would appear over the closing credits but, at Radiohead's instruction, wouldn't join "Talk Show Host" on the soundtrack album.

Exit music for a film, but entry music for an album: Yorke later told *Mojo*'s Jim Irvin that it was "the first performance we'd ever recorded where every note of it made my head spin – something I was proud of, something I could turn up really, really loud and not wince at any moment."

Recording sessions in July in their own studio in Oxfordshire were followed by September sessions at St Catherine's Court in Bath, Somerset, a 16th-century manor house owned by the actor Jane Seymour. Godrich – who was the same age as the band members and shared their "mindset", according to Thom – was by now firmly installed as their wingman, or unofficial sixth member, a position the producer would hold on every subsequent Radiohead album. By the end of the year, most of the recording was completed, with strings added at Abbey Road in London in January 1997.

By the time mixing was completed in early spring, *OK Computer* had taken Radiohead, in Thom's estimation, a year to make, although only three months of that was actual recording time – "in front of red lights", as he describes it to Jim Irvin in Barcelona. It's an image that evokes both stop signs and warning signs, neither of which sounds great for making an album but does speak to the state of the singer's frazzled sense of self.

Because – say it again – Barcelona is *a scrum*. At this point in late May 1997, likely none of those album reviews sampled at the top of this chapter have been published. But the word is out, the writing is on the wall and the world is wobbling on its axis.

On the day between the pair of shows at Zeleste, Thom talks to Jim of nerves the night before ("All the way through, yeah, every note") and the stress of promotion thereafter. "It's been a long time and all the stuff going on around us is really, really frightening and just trying to keep your head... I'm glad we did. All I know is the feeling afterwards of calm for the first time in months... Which of course has been completely fucked over today."

But there's no time to mope here at Ground Zero of Radiohead Phase #3. One month from now is Glastonbury, and it's a triumph. But on the same June day that in a boxing ring in Las Vegas Mike Tyson chomps a chunk of Evander Holyfield's ear in a WBA Heavyweight Championship bout, do Radiohead also bite off more than they can chew?

Reflecting on the band's live performances in the era/earache of *OK Computer*, "Glastonbury was the peak," Ed tells me in Japan four and a half years later. "Yeah, and then it was this gradual decline for the next eight months," Phil chips in. "It was a bit depressing, really."

Ed recalls, "Glastonbury was the twelfth gig [of the tour]. It was really weird. We were thrown into it, and had this very, very, very steep learning curve up to Glastonbury. Glastonbury drained us of all kinds of energy, emotion, whatever. The rest was just a war of attrition."

All that said, the guitarist, for his part, wasn't going to downplay the benefits of making an album that sold almost eight million physical copies, was acclaimed as one of the greatest of 1997 and won Best Alternative Music Album at the Grammys (it lost out on a Brit to The Verve's *Urban Hymns* and the Mercury Music Prize to *New Forms* by Roni Size/Reprazent). Before *The Bends*, in Ed's view, "we didn't fit into a category, we never fitted into the whole Britpop scene. That's where we felt happiest. Then suddenly with *OK Computer*, you're vying with The Verve for the album of 1997. But it's very flattering. You get seduced by it. However much you say, 'this is a freak, this isn't natural, this isn't right', you do get taken in by it all."

And onwards, ever onwards. Radiohead tour *OK Computer* until 18 April 1998, the date of the second of two shows at New York's Radio City Music Hall. Thom will later say the tour went on a year too long, which is a feat for a tour that lasted eleven months. Luckily, we have a record of that time-warping, head-spinning, eight-days-a-week period in the band's life.

Radiohead must have had a whiff of what their third album was going to do to their profile, because in Barcelona they already have a film crew in tow, chronicling this period of phoney war. Whether they could have anticipated what *OK Computer* would do to their *heads* and entire sense of self, individually and collectively, is another matter.

As Ed tells the man from *Musician*: "Nothing's been documented ever in our history, and this week is something we wanted to document." Asked why, the guitarist answers: "Don't you think it's unusual? We're in this beautiful city, and all these people have flown in just to see us. It's a pretty bizarre time."

Unusual and bizarre won't be the half of it. Because surely no one in their right minds would have seen rushes from Barcelona and then greenlit a film that would end up as a snuff movie for the age-old rock'n'roll dream of touring.

Director Grant Gee is on the ground in Spain, shooting, scurrying, capturing everything for a fly-on-the-wall... something. That, eventually, will become a tour documentary titled *Meeting People Is Easy*. The first footage in the film is of my *FACE* photographer buddy, Jake Chessum, grabbing what he can in the bogs. Tom's in there too, as he corralled the glum-boy-five in the streets outside.

From Barcelona to infinity and beyond... Or, at least, *The Late Show with David Letterman* in New York, where a frustrated Thom tussles with the talk show host's studio sound crew. It's an interlude typical of *Meeting People Is Easy*: a largely monochrome travelogue, a blurry collage of static and soundbites, of soundcheck snafus and backstage blow-outs, of press clippings and disembodied interview exchanges and mind-numbingly repetitious jousting matches with the world's press. There are some concerts and songs, too.

The interrogation is as endless as it is, often, witless. But, hey, rock hacks in glass houses...

"I want to know if you are aware of the fact that this album is going to be a classic?

"What is music to you?"

"What is music to you?"

"What is music?"

"Are you related in some way to the Britpop scene?"
(A sharp, gritted-teeth inhalation in answer to that one.)

"Is there anything that you want to do that you haven't done?"
("Oh lord," replies Thom.)

"What did you want to achieve when you started the band, what was your aim?"

"How do you define rock music?"

"Is there any influence from Genesis or Pink Floyd?" ("We all hate progressive rock music," Colin shoots back.)

"This record is incredible."

To the latter, the ever-drily-witty bass player responds: "One might say a lunatic, crazy act of desperate men."

To be clear: most of these exchanges are with scribblers who ADORE Radiohead. But the price of that love is that they want to understand, engage, dissect, get something new ("What would you say to Tom Cruise [if he came to a show]?"), offer their own theories.

"I [heard] a reason for it a couple of days ago," Thom says to one interviewer about another interviewer, "which is the best one yet: that *OK Computer* is about everything being out of control." Ironic snort not captured.

We hear a Spanish-accented interviewer ask the singer – over a background soundtrack of his "Paranoid Android" battered-angel wail of *"rain down on me, from a great height"* – what he's feeling about the likely reaction of an audience the following night.

"I'm terrified," replies Thom. Why? "Just 'cause, just coming back… it's sort of quite terrifying… just going into the whole… the wheels start turning again. And the industry starts moving again. This time bigger, more terrifying, and it just keeps going, basically outside of our control."

This, I'm guessing, is an exchange from Barcelona, from the phoney war before the "campaign" proper, and already the man at the front is feeling the burn. Cut to voiceover of, again, Thom I think, saying, with bleak cheerfulness, how "'Lucky' is actually wildly appropriate". Why? Because "we're standing on the edge," he says, quoting the song's closing lyric. As he says this, we watch Jonny strap into his wrist protector in a dressing room. Strap in, boys, buckle up and *brace*.

And on it goes.

"Punk Floyd" runs the headline in the Village Voice *on 26 August 1997. The caption under mug shots of Thom and Jonny: "Yorke and Greenwood: entering the rock elite".*

"I had a great conversation with Calvin Klein about underwear…" – Thom, lying, to celeb-anecdote-hungry American journo on tour bus.

"Radiohead! Creep! Dickhead!" – random male, American city street.

When it's released in November 1998, *Meeting People Is Easy* will reveal itself to be a 96-minute endurance test of eavesdropped interviews, wiretapped press conferences, hidden-camera revelations, dressing-room outbursts, ghostly voiceover, hotel rooms as prison cells, tour buses as sleek silver coffins. With occasional concerts and songs.

It's hard to believe that anyone involved in the undertaking could have conceived they would end up with a film that is the least-celebratory tour film ever. But they did. And, for better or worse*, *Meeting People Is Easy* will colour interviewers' perceptions of the band for years to come. By the time they're doing (scant, tactical) promotion for *Kid A* and *Amnesiac*, Phil will tell me that everyone the band encountered post-

OK Computer "did expect us to completely hate the whole process. And to be rather glum and inaccessible people." [*So, actually, worse.]

To quote the first viewer comment under a (possibly hooky) YouTube version of Gee's ultimately Grammy-nominated, half-a-million-selling, road-to-hell film: *"I've always considered this documentary to be a horror movie of sorts. There's a feeling of isolation and mental stress that makes the viewer feel alienated and let down. There's something frightening about seeing how the greatest band in the world was miserable after they released the greatest rock album of all time."*

Still, though, there were diamonds in the dark. Thom knew what they'd achieved with *OK Computer*, and what it meant. It might have nearly broken Radiohead but over that near-year-long world tour, he enjoyed enough human interactions to know how it had also helped fix fans.

On another interminable tour-bus night drive, he talks of listening, a lifetime ago, to LPs – The Smiths' *Strangeways, Here We Come*, R.E.M.'s *Dead Letter Office* – in the bedroom of a girl in Oxford. He can't believe that now, with *OK Computer*, Radiohead "evoke that thing of it being imprinted on your heart, every note of it.

"Everything else is bullshit. But that in itself is a reason to keep going – the idea that you form the most crucial part of someone's life, the nasty, nasty teenage bit, when everything goes completely wrong, ha ha!" concluded the man with the least-mirthful laugh in rock.

TOKYO:

Fast forward three and a half years. The band were big after the success of *The Bends* but hadn't gone fully nuclear. They were coming up to *OK Computer* territory; it wasn't out yet but there was a buzz starting to build about it. Albums used to be launched in Japan ahead of the rest of the world, and I was asked to go out there to join them and document the whole trip. It's a nice way of doing things, having me with them the whole time means that they don't end up having to do loads of photo sessions with all sorts of different people.

Thom had an idea of shooting the band in a big crowd, but looking totally anonymous. Which was a nice thought but didn't really work – once I go back 200 yards you can't bloody see anyone! We played around with the idea of anonymity though, and got some great shots of the band spread out a bit more, with Tokyo commuters going about their daily business in and around them. Even so, they still stood out like sore thumbs.

At the end of the four - or five-day trip it was Ed's birthday, so the record company booked out a room in a karaoke building. Everyone did a song,

APRIL 1997

but Thom absolutely brought the house down, closing the night out with an amazing take on Louis Armstrong's version of "What A Wonderful World". It was brilliant.

三千里薬品

むじんくんコーナー
3F
自動契約
コーナー
1F2F
KEN
KIRIN

みんなでなくそう放置駐車

アコム
JR

Panasonic
AVパソコン
新橋1号館
スプリングセール開催中

スプリングセール

グループ
待ち合わせにポケットベル
東京テレメッセージ
SEED
SUPER LISA SHIBUYA
NAGANO
Amway
297
NOW
東急ハンズ渋谷店
友達の恋人
トゥーランドット姫
Bunkamura シアターコクーン
東海銀行
案内図

BARCELONA:

After launching *OK Computer* in Japan, we went to Barcelona. It was same sketch, I was to go along and document the entire trip. Grant Gee was also there, filming things for what would eventually become the documentary, *Meeting People Is Easy* – in fact, I make a few cameo appearances in the film, you can hear my voice in the background a few times. It must have been such a draining experience for the band. Lots of waiting around, lots of commitments but always having to keep it rolling, keep it rolling.

You can see some of that frustration in the photographs, especially the ones of Thom sitting in a hotel foyer. He was waiting for the web chat in support of the album to kick off, which must have been one of the first of its kind but it never did end up working. But we did get out and about, on the streets and some rooftops, taking a trip to Gaudí's Park Güell as well. Of course, exhaustion sets in at some point, especially in the heat, but we were all there for a reason and the band knew that. It was good to keep them busy, if they stopped for a second they might think they were on holiday!

MAY 1997

GENERALITAT DE CATALUNYA
DEPARTAMENT DE JUSTÍCIA
P R E S E N T
Presentación Mundial de su ultimo album
OK COMPUTER
RADIOHEAD
against demons
against demons
Jueves 22 y Sábado 24 de Mayo
ZELESTE
Apertura de puertas 9 noche · RADIOHEAD 10 noche
COMPRA YA TUS ENTRADAS EN LOS SIGUIENTES PUNTOS
BARCELONA: DISCO 100 · REVOLVER · DISCOS GONG
OVERSTOCKS · PLANET MUSIC · HOSPITALET: DISCOMANIA · CORNELLÀ: COLLADO
COLOMA: JOCAR · MATARÓ: DISCOS BATLLE · TRAN · GRANOLLERS:
PAUL COLLINS
en concierto
PAUL COLLINS
PER OFFICE
MOBILIARI D'OFICINA

porta brace

TABACS
ESTRUCH

ABACS
Winston

ARTISTS

KILL ALL
ARTISTS

ARTISTS

Bus Turistic

B-0786-

GOLDERS GREEN LONDON:

The band were recording a session for BBC Radio 2, and I got a call from their publicist saying that Thom thought it would be a great idea for me to come over and capture it. I like the “work in progress” feel of the recording shots, they’re just busy doing their thing, working their magic and I’m there to document it, trying not to get in their way. They’re old hands at it by this point. I like the shots from above, where I must have been crawling about in a gallery or something and have called out to Thom to look up at me in between takes. But the other photographs show the reality of these sessions, without trying to varnish it. It’s a big messy room with blokes playing instruments.

I can see them reading newspapers in a few of the shots. That was the thing about Radiohead – whenever you went out to meet them anywhere, especially when they were abroad on tour, if you picked up a huge great big stack of all the latest papers to take out to them then you’d be the most popular person in the northern hemisphere. But then they wouldn’t talk to you, as they were busy reading!

MAY 1997

NO SMOKING
London's turning

VOX
Fender

BBC
88-91 FM
We Don't

88-91 FM
PREMiER

Some People
Talk About The
Weather.
We Don't

ATTACK No.1

VOX

VOX
23

THE ORCHARD

I went to meet the band in an old apple store – a store room for apples in an old orchard, not an apple store of the iPhone variety – which they had been using as a rehearsal space. I was shooting them for a *Melody Maker* front cover, and found them in this great old place, totally unpretentious, all dusty and dirty. There was a huge great tarpaulin lying around which was covered in paint, and which I thought would be the perfect ready-made backdrop. It was a Sunday afternoon but they knew what they had to do. It was a relaxed session, I knew the band by now so I just went along to meet them. I like the everyday feeling of the session. I noticed halfway through that Thom actually has a shopping list Tippexed on his hand, which isn't bit of stagecraft or direction from me – it's just his shopping list.

OXFORDSHIRE: MAY 1997

FICTION

FRANCE:

Radiohead were on tour, and I went to meet them in Strasbourg to shoot for *Time Out*. The band were always careful to take quality support acts with them – they'd already played with The Black Keys, Willy Mason – and this time they were with Sparklehorse.

Backstage, Thom wanted to try some shots where he was screaming and going kind of crazy into the lens. But I didn't feel comfortable supplying those images to the magazine. At that point in time, there was a narrative bubbling under in the press (who were fairly bloodthirsty for any kind of abnormality in any band) that Thom was a bit bonkers – which he absolutely wasn't. I didn't think this sequence would help that perception and so I held them back. I remember there was a feature in one of the music mags very early on in the band's career, basically making fun of how Thom looked when he was singing. It was out of order, it was mean and it made me feel quite protective of Thom and the band, especially as by this point I'd worked with them a lot and knew them fairly well. It fuelled me to try to do good by them with my photographs, particularly in the early days when the piece ran.

OCTOBER 1997

That slightly mean perception of Thom has passed now, it's a different world and so I'm pleased they're seeing the light of day – they're fun shots – but I wasn't comfortable with the idea at the time, and a different, more straightforward shot from that same sequence is the one that made the magazine cover.

SHAG

GERMANY:

This was a session for a magazine, probably a German one or possibly one of the Japanese mags. It made more sense for them to get someone like me, who knows the band, to shoot them rather than trying to get one of their own to start from scratch. This session is an interesting visual essay. The chaps are all looking at the lens and involved. I grabbed them around the soundcheck when there's a bit of waiting around anyway, and then stayed on to watch the show and rattle off some nice action shots.

NOVEMBER 1997

POUR LES

TION
5351POUR

WASHINGTON DC:

In mid-1998, Radiohead played the Tibetan Freedom Concert in Washington. I remember it was a total disaster to start with, the whole thing was rained off on the first day, a Saturday, with the band bumped to a slot the next day, if I recall. But they were obviously frustrated not to have done a show on that first day, and ended up playing an impromptu club gig that night. The first I heard of it was the next morning, when Colin asked why I hadn't made it! He'd phoned the hotel where everyone was staying and left a note for me to come and join them, but the cheapskates at my magazine had us staying somewhere else, out in Charlestown. So I never got the call, and missed the chance to see that one.

They did play their slot on the Sunday though, before Thom played a show the next day, as part of a rally in front of the Capitol Building. David Crosby was also on the bill that day, and Thom borrowed his guitar – you can see it in the photographs, with the Capitol Building making a great backdrop.

I remember Thom performing "Street Spirit (Fade Out)" at that show and it was incredible, unforgettable. I was almost moved to tears. I've been

JUNE 1998

lucky enough to see plenty of very talented musicians perform, but that was one that stopped me in my tracks, one of those times where you just freeze, listen and remember forever. I get goosebumps thinking about it.

ACTION FOR

NATIONAL

ON FOR

welcomes you

GREECE + GERMANY:

I joined the band in Athens, after a three-year gap since my last session with them. After they'd played a show there I remember we travelled from Greece to Berlin the next morning, and Thom and Jonny decided that they were going to get the train, rather than travel on the tour bus – so I said, I'll go with you guys! Much more civilised. I was on the trip to document it, and of course the band didn't want to be photographed at 8.30 in the morning on a train platform, but thankfully they obliged me as I think they're interesting shots.

I shot their sound check ahead of a show with a panoramic XPan camera, which gives a nice wide view without any distortion. You can see the band are relaxed and laughing, which despite the image they sometimes project is exactly how I remember them. There was already a bit of humour flying around, which I found very endearing. But then bang, with the flick of a switch they're into some of the greatest, deepest music ever made. It's incredible really. In the same way, I love the dressing room pictures of the Greenwood brothers. It's how I remember them. If Jonny's not playing guitar or fiddling with

JUNE 2000

switches and dials then he's reading. He never wastes time. None of the band do. They devour culture, which makes them inspiring to be around.

ΑΘΗΝΑΙ (ΠΕΙΡΑΙΕΥΣ)
ΚΑΤΕΡΙΝΗ - ΛΑΡΙΣΣΑ
ΛΕΙΑΝΟΚΛΑΔΙΟΝ - ΘΗΒΑΙ

IGNORE
ALIEN
ORDERS

MAIN
V1

Fender
PRECISION BASS

TOKYO:

It's 2am, or thereabouts, on a tiny stage in a small room on the seventh floor of a tower block in the Japanese capital's drinking neighbourhood of Roppongi – and it's karaoke o'clock.

It's a year and a day since the release of *Kid A*. Four months and four days since the release of *Amnesiac*. One month and nine days until the release of *I Might Be Wrong: Live Recordings*. But three albums in 13 months – a triple-whammy, double-Grammy triumph after the two most arduous years of Radiohead's existence (and that's saying something) – is no reason to break out the Barry Manilow.

But the end of an elongated, stretched-out tour that was sometimes in-tents but only occasionally (really) intense? With everyone on smiling terms? Now those are reasons for celebration. It's time for Ed O'Brien to get his "Copacabana" on.

These are the third-last and penultimate shows on the tour in support of Radiohead's fourth and fifth studio albums, recorded concurrently over 16 difficult months in studios in England, Denmark and France. The roads and miles that subsequently brought us here to Tokyo began in Europe almost a year and a half earlier, in summer 2000, in Roman amphitheatres, a royal villa, a 100-year-old Neo-Rococo theatre and the continent's largest cinema.

Tom Sheehan was there in Greece and Germany as the band challenged fans head-on with a brace of unreleased songs: opening their set with the turbulence of "Optimistic". Spasming into the limber funk (or was it free jazz?) of "The National Anthem". Keening the Tony Blair-baiting spectral shiver-punk of "You and Whose Army?" (a song about, Thom tells *Uncut*, "anybody who is put in a position of power and is then surrounded by his cronies and goes off and does this thing and doesn't feel that he's answerable to anybody"). Unveiling without flourish "Everything in Its Right Place", the mantric techno-hymn that will, eventually, as the opening track on *Kid A*, put down a marker for Radiohead Phase #4.

Those in attendance on the continent that summer who had heard the rumours that Radiohead – in recovery from the attrition of the *OK Computer* campaign and beset by civil war in their long months in various studios – had melted down their guitars and turned them into Ondes Martenots now had early proof. The band had indeed gone electronic and gone rogue. Courtesy of Napster, everyone else immediately had proof, too.

Those Wild West days of illegal file-sharing explained the ultra-fastidious – you might say fussy – way in which *Kid A* was distributed to reviewers ahead of its release in October 2000. It was only listenable to via a new (and very short-lived) form of audio device – a chunky, felt-tip-pen-shaped contraption with no speaker and earphones glued into the jack. Also, the band wouldn't be doing any interviews. Oh, and there would be no singles.

Unfortunately, for some this anti-promotional "stance", not to mention the technological faffery, only served to underscore what they saw as self-importance within the music, viz *Melody Maker*'s review:

"So earthbuggering is the event of Radiohead deigning to record some music that review samples are distributed on uncopiable, non-uploadable 'listening sticks' to prevent this most mercurial of music from falling into the wrong hands, then being whacked on to www.copyrightinfringementagogo.com and exposed to the public at large as the tubby, ostentatious, self-congratulatory, look-ma-I-can-suck-my-own-cock whiny old rubbish it is... It is the sound of Thom Yorke ramming his head firmly up his own arse, hearing the rumblings of his intestinal wind and deciding to share it with the world."

What larks. What Luddites.

Little wonder that, in Japan 366 days after its release, Thom, a few days shy of his thirty-third birthday, reflects, not-entirely-unhappily, that "it was like we set off a stink bomb."

OCTOBER 2001

And what a stench it was. *Kid A* entered the UK charts at Number One, and also became the band's first American Number One album. Like *OK Computer*, it won the Grammy for Best Alternative Music Album. Then, with *Amnesiac* (a Grammy-winner for Best Recording Package), Radiohead doubled-down. Then, with *I Might Be Wrong*, tripled down.

Radiohead had ripped it up and started again – again. No one in the band was going to pretend it had been easy. No one was going to lie and say they were entirely satisfied with how in-band politicking had been conducted during those 16 arduous studio months. But via the funky funk of their "stink bomb" and bloody-minded experimentation – and via, still, whatever the naysayers said, great songwriting – they had successfully liberated themselves. From *OK Computer*-mania. From expectation. From the very idea of what being a Rock Band (genus: *giganticus*) entailed.

So here, now, in the wee hours in Tokyo, they're celebrating. Six hours earlier, Ed was on stage at the Budokan Arena, all gyrating hips and flexing wrists as he worked raspy percussion at the beginning of "Paranoid Android". Now he's doing his best Manilow and making exactly the same slinky moves.

Phil Selway is next. He takes the karaoke mic for his song, Take That's "Back for Good". The assembled gathering, high on jugs of diluted lager and pokey tequila, applaud wildly. Phil can sing! (Of course he can, but it will take the best part of a decade from now, and a rebrand as Philip, for him to start releasing solo albums.)

We are denied the opportunity to savour Colin Greenwood's predilection for karaoke Joy Division. Despite his reputation for being last out of the bar, any bar, the bass player has already returned to the hotel, annoyed at the dithering over where the party was going next. There's no Jonny Greenwood – karaoke "is just not his thing", Phil says. "Unless he could do it through his effects pedal," Ed chuckles.

And there's no Thom either, so we're denied the pleasure of the singer's rendition of Louis Armstrong's "What a Wonderful World" – a performance of which had many of the Japanese record company in tears last time Radiohead were in the country.

Earlier, though, Thom cheerfully joined the throng at the aftershow in one of the conference rooms strung along the Budokan's circular perimeter. It was a gathering of the type made infamous by the bands-are-hell, touring-is-hellish *Meeting People Is Easy* documentary. But everyone was smiling, Radiohead seemingly happy to mill around, chat to old acquaintances and drink plastic cups of champagne purloined by their manager. After a couple of hours everyone packed up, Thom nonchalantly stuffing a bottle of vodka into one of his shopping bags.

This is where Radiohead have chosen to end their world tour. This week they set the seal on three albums and 18 revolutionary months. They must be in something of a good mood because, well, they've let me come to Japan and interview them for a feature for *THE FACE*. And they've barely talked to any press in the last year.

So: how was it for them?

"We understand more now what we're doing than when we were doing *OK Computer*. We understand more why we decided to carry on because we had to question everything. And," Thom says with a champagne-loosened smile, "what doesn't kill you makes you stronger!"

*

Thom, Jonny and Colin are sitting in a minibus, swigging fizz. When I point out that it's a year since the release of *Kid A*, Thom is bamboozled: "Really? Jesus. It feels like about 10 years to me."

Asked for their perspective on that time, Colin muses that, "looking back on it now, I have this perverse desire to release singles off *Kid A* just so people could hear it. Not because we were being perverse at the time..."

The bass player thinks people were "disappointed" by the album. Thom thinks "they were pretty angry. They were in Britain, anyway." Their upset, reasons Colin, is because *Kid A* "wasn't like *OK Computer* [but] with bigger tunes and stadium potential".

Thom, though, insists he's not disappointed by that response. "Not really. Because everyone else in the band was like: 'Well, this was gonna happen.' In a bizarre sort of way there's a sense of relief, because the pressure's off."

"Some people wanted us to sound like the bands that sound a bit like us," Jonny pipes up, "but better."

"And that's really sad," says Colin.

As the clock ticks past midnight and, maybe, who knows, the champagne takes hold, Thom 'fesses up.

"I had an agenda when we started recording, which was impossible to live up to. I'm not even quite sure what it was."

Was it, I venture, reinventing the band?

"Oh, yeah. Completely, yeah. But it was essentially quite a destructive way of approaching anything. What was happening in the studio was despite everything, in a way. We'd leave sessions and go: 'What the fuck happened there?' Then go back a few weeks later and go: 'Oh my God, this is great!'

"That's been the weird thing about going out and playing live: remembering that the best thing about being in a band and making music is responding to the moment, and things growing of their own accord. The less you fuck with them sometimes, the better." That said, the singer adds, "sometimes you do need to put a spanner in the works."

Leaning in and digging in as we sit parked outside their hotel, Thom gives some credence to the rumours that, in the long months after the epically draining *OK Computer* phase, when the band were burrowed in studios, with guitarist Ed and drummer Phil and bass player Colin often left twiddling their thumbs as the electronic experimentation ran away with itself, the cracks within the band were widening perilously.

"To be perfectly honest, we weren't really sure–" Thom stops, restarts. "To me it was a miracle that we finished the material on the record. It was a miracle that everything stuck together. it was a miracle that we got our shit together. It was a miracle that we picked up the pieces after *OK Computer*. And everything after that was just a fucking bonus, really," Thom says, brightening, "a Number One bonus card!"

The week they were at Number One in America and Britain with *Kid A*, he received many calls at his New York hotel. "Endless messages, all saying: 'You better fucking enjoy this! If you don't deal with this, you're the saddest!'"

That same week, they played *Saturday Night Live*.

"That was my highlight of the year," says Yorke vigorously. "Because we played really well. And the versions we did of 'Idioteque' and 'The National Anthem'... For me it was like being a child and somebody saying: 'You have 10 minutes of television in America, completely live, no gaps, and you can do whatever the fuck you like and there will be x millions of people watching!'

"And I was really, really excited about it. And then just at the last minute before we went on, Michael Stipe turned up, and he was really geeing me up. But he gave me all these terrible warnings about how horrific it was. But I was surprised that *Saturday Night Live* meant so much to me."

Then – via summer 2021's triumphant US tour, a homecoming concert for 44,000 in Oxford's South Park and more European shows – Japan. And now, finally, it's nearly home time.

The day after the Budokan show, Radiohead travel the hour or so to Yokohama by bus. Their final two gigs will be in the town's arena. Thom's piano tuner has been and gone. Now, in an empty arena in the afternoon, their sound man is testing the PA with a series of computer farts. *Hrrrr bloop bleep fizz rrrt...*

"Oh yeah, I've got that record," deadpans Thom, centre stage, into his microphone. More noises. "On that Berlin label, isn't it?" jokes the self-aware man who knows that, for a year now, rockist scribes have been taking the piss out of his love for Aphex Twin and the collected works of Sheffield electronic label Warp.

Radiohead soundcheck with "Knives Out" and a new tune with no name and mumbled words. It is a clanging, driving thing, a bit Doors-like, full of swampy blues riffs. In Seattle, they played another new song that they're calling "The Reckoner". Yorke describes it as "like a heavy metal tune. It will be absolutely brilliant. I've got this thing in my head, I know it's gonna be amazing, but it's absolutely miles away." Indeed, it is absolutely miles away: the song, retitled "Reckoner" and radically reworked, will finally break cover on their 2007 album, *In Rainbows*.

After soundcheck, band and crew gather together for an end-of-term group photo. Then Phil and Ed settle down in a quiet room off the catering area and reflect on matters of scale.

"When we first did arenas on *OK Computer*, we had over 50 people in our crew. Part of you felt, hey, we deserve this! But then you get embarrassed. We are not worthy of this! We didn't feel comfortable doing Wembley. [So] it's been really nice to have a lot of negative press – it's good for us!"

"You just feel like a huge fraud," nods Phil.

Phil thinks they "definitely" overthought *Kid A* and *Amnesiac*. Ed goes back to the importance of "the ability to be throwaway. It just frees you up. But the more successful you become, the more people hang on Thom's every word. If you're throwaway, you can be a lot more daring."

When I suggest that the records are seen as much as experiments in sounds as records, Ed nods. "I think the criticism levelled at *Kid A* on an emotional level is absolutely fair enough. We were so inhibited, so scared of letting go in the studio, partly because of the 'rock' tag. Because what we associated with rock was letting go, and the emotional *bleeeurgh*, a real change."

The result of all of which is: Radiohead are thrilled with being Radiohead in a manner unseen since the release of *The Bends* in 1995. In this regard, *Kid A*, *Amnesiac* and *I Might Be Wrong* have done their job. Band manager Bryce Edge says he's never seen Radiohead this happy at this stage of a world tour before. Normally, agree the band, they can't look each other in the eye by tour's end. The feeling within the band now is variously described as "buoyant" (Phil), "the best touring experience we've ever had" (Ed), "jetlagged" (Colin), "tight" (Thom) and "I'm trying to think of a nice word..." (Jonny).

Radiohead play two nights at Yokohama, then go their separate ways. The first of these shows, the one I see, is fantastic. "Idioteque" is a stand-out. As 1995's "Talk Show Host" later emerged as an important transitional song, giving them a compass reading for the direction of *Kid A*, so "Idioteque" is cited by the band as a way forward. Lean, dry and reliant on studio effects on record, they had to find a way to make it work in concert. Now, live, it's limber, propulsive, emotional, energetic. Techno-soul.

Radiohead plan to reconvene next summer for rehearsals. They will do three weeks of "scaled-down" shows in August 2002 to road-test new material – "to let people [in the band] get their shit together," in the words of Jonny.

Will they play Glastonbury?

"I'm not allowed to say (anything about) that!" fudges Ed. "The idea is that we don't want to do anything big. The idea is to be pretty self-indulgent – that means we'll play new material. And I don't think playing Glastonbury, or any festival, is conducive to that..."

Then they'll go into the studio to record their sixth studio album, with a view to an early 2003 release date. "We'll keep it fairly brief," says the guitarist. "And not get too... too *cerebral* about the whole thing."

Thom has been giving his bandmates tapes of ideas for new songs. This is a good sign, says Bryce. Ahead of the recording of *Kid A/Amnesiac*, for the first time in the band's history, he didn't do this. And there are going to be a *lot more* tapes passed around, too, Yorke says. He and Jonny are going back to what they did with *OK Computer*, working on turning half-formed ideas into more substantial ideas.

"We wanna do that thing like ABBA. Like Benny and the other bloke."

"Am I Benny?" Jonny wonders. "You've got the beard."

"Yeah, yeah," says face-fuzzy Thom eagerly. "With the beards, in the hut. They used to go in there every day and write."

Can the singer describe the feel of the new songs?

"No, absolutely not. I really, really can't. Because there's four or five areas of different– Well, it's like where we are, really. Where we are is, we're still very, very into what we're doing with the computers, even though we've been touring for ages. Especially you," he says, looking at Jonny, "and me – we're still heavily into computer stuff. Jonny's heavily into his analogue wires and cables. But also, there's a really concerted effort to use the songwriting thing again."

At the same time, though, "my ambition in life is just to make a record that's just... funky. Makes you want to have sex."

Hail to the chief: Thom Yorke is back. I can't speak to whether he's having sex. But he is having fun.

HOLBORN STUDIOS LONDON:

This session, shot for *Uncut* magazine, was a laugh. The chaps were fed up with doing band photo sessions. They were already shooting something for another magazine in Holborn Studios in London. They weren't doing much press, and their office didn't want to do anything for *Uncut* as well. But, as my old mother used to say, there's more than one way to skin a cat. Since I knew them and their team I said to Jonesy, Editor of *Uncut*, leave it to me. I got on to their PR and suggested I do a few minutes with each band member in Studio 10 while they're on their way to Studio 1, just down the corridor, and have each member for just five minutes. Eventually, we went ahead, each of them was wheeled in one at a time and I photographed them all individually, quick as you like, and then worked on painstakingly comping them together to get a single portrait the old-fashioned way, on the enlarger like we did in the pre-digital days. It actually works nicely because you can focus on each member in turn. I love the photographs of Thom in his duffle coat, very mysterious, isolated, "leave me alone".

APRIL 2001

ZEPPO

ZEPPO

ZEPPO

ZEPPO

BRISTOL/OXFORD/LONDON:

There, there: little boy lost Thom Yorke is yomping – slowly – through Fifty Acre Wood, five miles west of Bristol. The artist most recently known as the most back-to-frontman in music is making a pop video – and with noticeable good cheer. Take after take, yomp after yomp, as filmmaker Chris Hopewell captures slo-mo footage for the hand-crafted, stop-motion fantasia he and his team are fashioning to promote "There, There", the pounding, energizing first single from Radiohead's sixth album, *Hail to the Thief*.

Later today, against a green screen in an animation studio in Bristol, Thom will have to use only his upper body to mime running – at one-third real-time – while being attacked by a murder of crows. Then he must pretend he's wearing boots, which, as if by magic, take over his legs and enable him to escape the birds. Anyone who's been mesmerized by Thom's particularly antic dancing onstage will recognize the flailing and the wincing.

He's been doing this for three days, and there's another one to go. Then the animators will spend two weeks speeding up his slowed-down movements and integrating them with puppet sections featuring a party of pipe-smoking squirrels in their parlour, kittens having a tea party in the hollowed-out base of a tree, and the angry crows.

Film buff Thom had been keen to use Darren Aronofsky, visionary director of *Pi* and *Requiem for a Dream*, to make this video. But the songwriter, who always felt that "There, There" was like a "kids' fairy tale", decided the Canadian auteur's script "was a bit flat". A few coincidences and phone calls later, Team Radiohead ended up talking to Bristol's Collision Films.

"Thom gave me a brief saying it should be a bit Brothers Grimm, a bit [Czech animation legend Jan] Švankmajer," says Hopewell. "It's fifties' East-European genre animation, overlaboured and naive."

"It's Bagpuss," says Thom, referring to the "saggy old cloth cat" whose titular children's stop-motion animation was a staple of a British seventies' childhood.

Standing in amongst the trees, watching Thom happily make a fool of himself, is Dilly Gent. She's worked with Radiohead from the days of *Pablo Honey*, commissioning a series of landmark videos, notably the ones that accompanied the singles from *The Bends* and *OK Computer* (*see*: "Street Spirit (Fade Out)" and "Karma Police", both directed by Jonathan Glazer). She left their record company, Parlophone, three years before, and is a freelance "visual consultant" for the band. This means she's involved with their videos, photoshoots and any live filming.

Dilly is telling Radiohead's press officer of a conversation she had with a Parlophone employee who works with another band signed to the label. "I'd never get [Frontman X] to do this," the astonished former colleague had said on learning that Thom had committed to a four-day shoot. "That's so good!"

Dilly had replied with a sanguine, "Thom knows how important this is."

Here, in 2003, Radiohead are a changed band, something *The Daily Telegraph* – for whom I'm interviewing them – will drill into in the cover-line for my story in the newspaper's Saturday magazine: "Turn on, tune in, cheer up – how Thom Yorke and Radiohead got their groove back."

Certainly, they remain fiercely clever, politically sussed and immaculately principled. But they're no longer the angst-ridden, grim-faced, artsy bunch of obscure musos of popular myth. Although that, being a myth, was never their real deal anyway, as attested by mine and the band's last, karaoke'n'champagne-fuelled interaction in Tokyo. But the fact that they're currently presenting as more chilled than, say, the fast-rising Coldplay (aka Radiohead for children) is one indication. A listen to the pacey, economical *Hail to the Thief* – recorded in Los Angeles in a fast fortnight and set for release three months from now – is another.

APRIL 2003

The first thing you hear is the sound of a guitar being plugged in, then Thom saying, "that's a nice way to start". Then producer Nigel Godrich murmuring "rolling". Then Jonny Greenwood's analogue synthesizer – "a huge box that we use as a drum machine," explains Colin Greenwood, "that makes four noises and has flashing lights and that's like a Heath Robinson tea-maker" – barks into life. And we're off.

There are tunes, big ones. Loud guitars. Lyrics you can hear, and understand. In the songs "Sail To The Moon" and "I Will", classic Radiohead-style ballads in the mould of "Lucky" and "No Surprises". In Colin's summation: "For me, the big thing about the record is Thom's voice and singing. I love the lyrics, and I love the fact that you can hear all the words to the songs... There's a lot of humour in the lyrics, slapstick or knockabout or whatever. And vituperation.... He's gone for having the light shone on things and I think has found more room for manoeuvre because of it, rather than feeling more restricted."

There are other signs of light. For *Kid A*, no singles meant, obviously, no videos. Instead, they commissioned three directors to make 72 "blipverts" of between 10 and 42 seconds' length. For *Amnesiac*, the band did agree to shoot two videos, for "Pyramid Song" and "Knives Out". But they weren't in the former, and they hated the latter, so it was hardly seen anywhere.

Now, though, it seems Radiohead are willing to promote – dare I say, sell – themselves again...

"Fuck yeah!" exclaims Thom. "I'm trying to persuade the record company to shell out on lots of singles and all that stuff. This is a pop record. It's really direct. It has this energy to it. I'd love to know that it was on the radio. Great! Just 'cause that's where my head's at. I don't want to be on the top shelves at the back. 'Cause I'm into it too much. I like it. It is," he repeats, just in case I had trouble believing him (I did), "pop music."

The week before Bristol, I rendezvous with Thom, 34, in the Oxford branch of mid-market brasserie chain Café Rouge, a short drive from the Oxfordshire home he shares with girlfriend Rachel and their two-year-old son Noah. The last time we'd met, in Tokyo, a year-and-a-half earlier, he told me he next wanted to make a sex-positive funk album (or words to that effect). Now he says that, post-*Kid A* and *Amnesiac* the band considered "what kind of lurch in another direction are we gonna take now, you know, unexpectedly, ra ra ra?" This is a Thom tic: taking the mick out of himself, and also out of the media's snarky view of Radiohead's "ways".

"And, um, that was kind of doing my head in for a while," he continues. "I took a long six months off. Then my girlfriend said: 'Why don't you just do a record where you let it happen? Just go in and do it. No agenda, nothing.' And that sort of made things click."

In contrast to the intense, divisive, Thom-driven conceptualizing and creation of *Kid A* and *Amnesiac*, the making of *Hail to the Thief* has been characterized by the frontman loosening up and opening up. "I just totally relied on everyone else's judgement. I let go. No one was driving at all, really. Nigel was, in the sense that he was behind the tape machine and recording it. But really it was [a case of]: 'Let it happen and let it just drop off the cliff.'" He means in a good way.

Before they began recording, Thom tells me, Ed asked him to compile a CD for the guitarist of the singer's new, work-in-progress material. Specifically: "Can you do me a CD of all the songs that are just *songs*?" Thom is still tickled by this. And while he might not care to admit it, he knew exactly what Ed meant.

"Around *Kid A*, we didn't want to compete," Ed tells me. That is: we're not playing the same game as Coldplay and which meant, amongst other things, non-song songs. "We didn't want to participate. *Bang*," the guitarist says, verbalizing their explosive stance, "we're Radiohead and we're doing our own thing."

But as he also says, "one of the commandments of being in Radiohead is: 'You shall not go over old territory.'" So, from disengagement to engagement. From non-songs back to songs again.

I'm speaking to the rest of Radiohead in a Victoriana-themed hotel in Kensington, West London, a few days after talking to Thom. In terms of making their sixth album, I ask Ed for his version of "just going in and doing it" with "no agenda, nothing".

"Get it over quickly," he replies. "Be direct. I was sick of the haze of *Amnesiac*. *Kid A* was brilliant, *Amnesiac* wasn't that good. That left a bit of a nasty aftertaste... Most of all, I wanted energy. We haven't had energy like there is on this record since *The Bends*. *OK Computer* was getting a little bit..." He grins. "We probably started smoking a lot more grass!"

And as for Jonny, what did he set out to achieve with *Hail to the Thief*?

"To use computers in a different way," the younger Greenwood says. "I was one of the generation that grew up with the ZX Spectrum, and I always felt like computers were taken away from me as soon as Macs and PCs came along. I found a low-level music software: Max MSP. It's used in universities to teach electronic music... I imagined myself working for Roland in 1979 and having to decide what a drum kit sounds like. It's so low level, it's great. And you obviously end up with things that nobody else has done yet, or would want to do. I'm really in love with that side of electronic music now. It's been really liberating. So, there's lots of that on the album."

Phil Selway, too, speaks of liberation, and of the rediscovered openness within the new model Radiohead.

"For Radiohead to work properly, we have to communicate properly. And we've all taken responsibility for that this time, making sure we're as direct and open as we can be. When those elements haven't been there in the past, and we've been very English about it and sat on top of stuff, it's really slowed up the process and made it quite a painful process to go through."

Was making *Hail to the Thief* a, well, happier process?

"Yes," the drummer says emphatically. "It had to be, really. I don't think we could have gone through another session like the ones for *Kid A* and *Amnesiac*. What got us through those sessions was a great sense that we'd shed a load of baggage halfway through. Then we could regain the enthusiasm for making music. With the *Hail to the Thief* sessions, there was a confidence, an enthusiasm, about what we were doing. There was also a spontaneity about it, which certainly hadn't been there for quite a while."

Enthusiasm, spontaneity, humour... and bite. As Colin touched on with his talk of "vituperation", *Hail to the Thief* is also angry. Here, in spring 2003, we're a month or so into the new world disorder characterized by the American-led invasion of Iraq. Shortly before he went down to the woods today, Thom attended a peace rally at RAF Fairford in Gloucestershire, home of American B-52 bombers. "America is being run by a bunch of religious maniac bigots who stole their election," he told the crowd of 2,000, "and their only way of retaining power is to wage war."

The slogan "hail to thief" was chanted by demonstrators at George W. Bush's inauguration, a reference to his having "stolen" the presidency in 2000 from the numerically more popular Al Gore. But despite what he said at RAF Fairford, Thom insists the album title is not directed at POTUS #43 – and that it's not a political album.

"It will annoy me if people say it's a direct protest because I feel really strongly that we didn't write a protest record, we didn't write a political record." What he will allow, however, is "the fact that the music was positive and has all this energy gave me licence to write the lyrics that I wrote. It was only when I got to the end of it I realized how angry it was. All the way through the record there is this sense of trying to understand how one human being can make a decision and affect thousands of other people's lives. Our glorious leader, for example," he says, witheringly, of Tony Blair. "He thinks, believes, that he's doing the right thing over this war, when he's not being presented with the facts or he's choosing to ignore the consequences..."

For Thom Yorke, that anger isn't going away anytime soon. The next album he will release after *Hail to the Thief* is 2006's *The Eraser*. His first solo album is a record spitting with rage about environmental degradation and the Iraq War, and the latter's generationally-defining tragic consequences – not least the suicide of British weapons inspector Dr David Kelly. The government scientist was embroiled in a scandal over a "dodgy dossier" about Iraqi weapons of mass destruction that the Blair government used to justify the UK joining the American invasion. His body is found in Oxfordshire woodland a month after the release of *Hail to the Thief*.

On top of that: Thom will later tell me that, by 2004 (only one year after the release of *Hail to the Thief*), life in Radiohead "was getting boring and it just got a bit weird and self-perpetuating... It felt like everyone was under obligation to do it rather than because we wanted to do it. And one of the things I had wanted to do for ages was get stuck into a bunch of things that I had been mucking around with that didn't fit into the Radiohead zone."

Cue *The Eraser*. And cue, the year after that, *In Rainbows*: Radiohead's revolutionary, paradigm-shifting, pay-what-you-want-to-download seventh album from 2007. Nothing boring or self-perpetuating about that because–

Well, let's not get ahead of ourselves. We're in spring 2003 and the sun is shining. Three months from now, in the week of the release of *Hail to the Thief*, Radiohead will be in New York with Tom Sheehan. They just can't get rid of the guy. But who better to document radio sessions being recorded at Electric Lady Studios and a show at the Beacon Theatre?

It is, again, another pivotal time for the band, because coming up is Glastonbury, again, a second headline slot, six years to the day since that muddy brilliant *OK Computer*-era victory. They are Radiohead and they are, nine years since Tom first shot them in Oxford, at the top of their game, still.

Hail to the chiefs.

NYC:

I flew out to New York to meet the band and document their trip. They were in town to play Field Day, an open-air festival. It was absolutely pissing it down with rain but they played a great show. I was there to document the open-air show, a radio recording in Electric Ladyland studios and a performance they did in a theatre for MTV. It's always quite tricky to get shots in on trips like this, you need to act on the hoof and grab things when you can. You can't shoot much when the band are recording as you don't want your camera shutter to be picked up, and when they have some downtime and are spending their time reading they want to be left in their zone, which you have to respect. On the last day we did hatch a plan to go onto the roof of the Mercer, the hotel in Greenwich Village we were staying in, but the continuing rain meant that we had to abandon that and instead took some shots in the massive room Phil had somehow ended up staying in.

The shows they played were brilliant as ever, and I remember a really nice moment that, for me, summed up the band and their supportive spirit. It was during soundcheck at the theatre, things weren't quite going smoothly with the sound and

JUNE 2003

Thom was beginning to get quite frustrated with the sound quality. Ed just walked over to him, wrapped his arms around Thom in a big hug, and then took off his guitar and walked him offstage. I remember it as a lovely moment, one that summed up the care and love that they have for each other.

Design by Carl Glover at Aleph Studio

First published in 2024 by Welbeck
An imprint of HEADLINE PUBLISHING GROUP

1

Cataloguing in Publication Data is available from the British Library

ISBN: 9781802798012
Printed and bound in Italy

Headline's policy is to use papers that are natural, renewable and recyclable products and made from wood grown in well-managed forests and other controlled sources. The logging and manufacturing processes are expected to conform to the environmental regulations of the country of origin.

HEADLINE PUBLISHING GROUP
An Hachette UK Company
Carmelite House
50 Victoria Embankment
London EC4Y ODZ

www.headline.co.uk
www.hachette.co.uk